The WARLORD'S KITES

The WARLORD'S KITES

Virginia Walton Pilegard
Illustrated by Nicolas Debon

PELICAN PUBLISHING COMPANY
Gretna 2004

To my editor, Nina Kooij, and to Pam Albers, Stephanie Williams, and all women who help each other fly the kites of their dreams—V. W. P.

To Nathalie Bachelier—N. D.

Copyright © 2004
By Virginia Walton Pilegard

Illustrations copyright © 2004
By Pelican Publishing Company, Inc.

The word "Pelican" and the depiction of a pelican are trademarks of Pelican Publishing Company, Inc., and are registered in the U.S. Patent and Trademark Office.

Library of Congress Cataloging-in-Publication Data

Pilegard, Virginia Walton.
   The warlord's kites / by Virginia Walton Pilegard ; illustrated by Nicolas Debon.
      p. cm.
   Summary: When a hostile army attacks the warlord's palace in ancient China, Chuan and his friend, Jing Jing, find an ingenious way to scare them off using simple kites. Includes instructions for making a kite from a paper bag.
   ISBN 1-58980-180-6 (hardcover : alk. paper)
   [1. Kites—Fiction. 2. China—History—To 221 B.C.—Fiction.] I. Debon, Nicolas, ill. II. Title.

PZ7.P6283Waqf 2004
[E]—dc22

                           2003027661

Printed in Singapore
Published by Pelican Publishing Company, Inc.
1000 Burmaster Street, Gretna, Louisiana 70053

THE WARLORD'S KITES

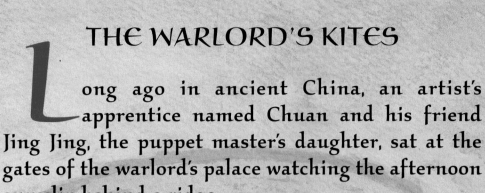

Long ago in ancient China, an artist's apprentice named Chuan and his friend Jing Jing, the puppet master's daughter, sat at the gates of the warlord's palace watching the afternoon sun slip behind a ridge.

Across an open field, they spied a rapidly moving cloud of dust. As it came closer, they could see the horses and riders of an approaching army.

"Cowards! They dare to challenge us because my father is away," the warlord's oldest son cried from atop the wall. "Shut the gates."

Chuan and Jing Jing rushed to help push the heavy gates closed. Within moments the sounds of shouting men, squealing horses, and pounding hooves surrounded the palace.

"**O**pen and we might let you live," the leader of the horsemen bellowed. "Our walls are strong," the warlord's son told the people in the courtyard. "We will wait them out."

When darkness came, Chuan climbed the wall to see
soldiers lighting campfires. Unable to sleep, he crept
into the artist's workshop, gathered pieces of sandalwood bark and
handfuls of rice straw, and carried them outside to his master's vat
of clear spring water to begin the long process of making paper.

"Have you ever made a paper kite?" Jing Jing's soft voice startled him. He turned to see her staring at the strips of sun-whitened paper he had hung to dry some days ago.

"No, but I have seen many kites." Chuan wondered why she had followed him. Perhaps she too was having trouble resting.

"Could you measure paper to make a square kite?" She gestured with her hands.

C huan pushed the last piece of bark beneath the water and squatted on his heels. "I have studied *Nine Chapters on the Mathematical Art*," he said. He watched her face to see if she were impressed. "If you can tell me why I should waste paper on kites, I can measure the area of any square you desire."

"I know a way to save the palace," she said. "I need just three kites."

The warlord's son strolled past. "We could tie Chuan to a big kite and sail him up to spy on the enemy," he offered with a grin. "A famous general once used that technique to win a war."

"We don't need a spy," Jing Jing said. "We can see the soldiers all too well, and their plans are hardly a secret."

"Unfortunately, you are right." The warlord's son turned away. "I must check with the servants to see how much food we have stored in the palace."

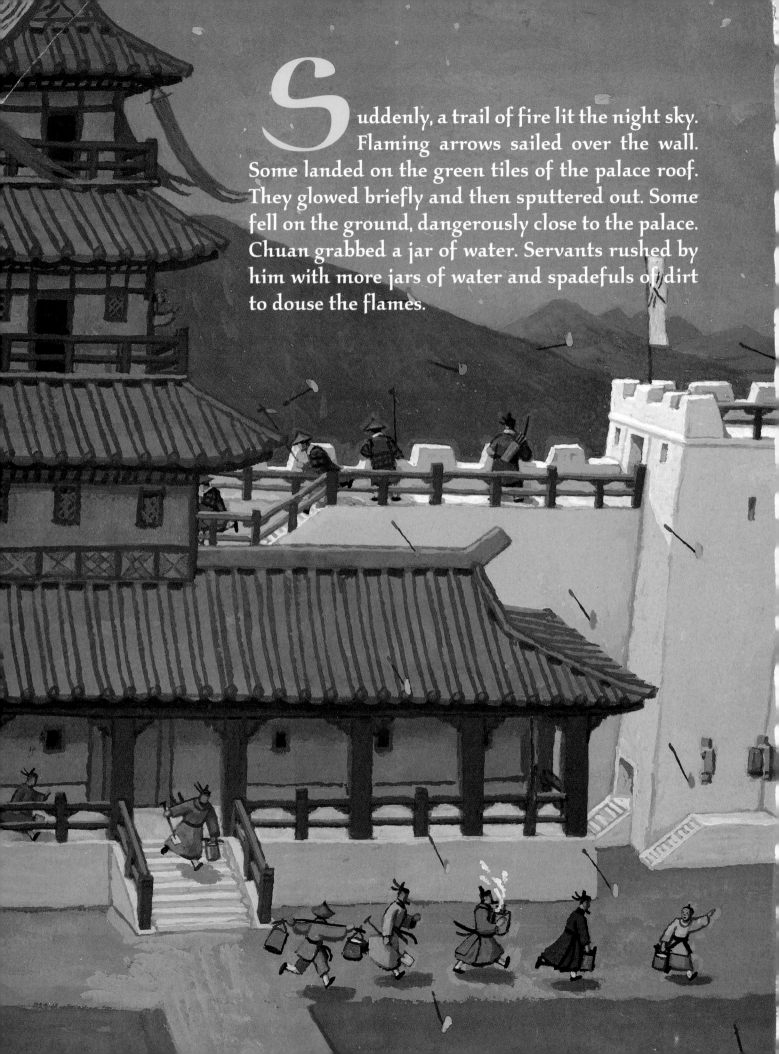

Suddenly, a trail of fire lit the night sky. Flaming arrows sailed over the wall. Some landed on the green tiles of the palace roof. They glowed briefly and then sputtered out. Some fell on the ground, dangerously close to the palace. Chuan grabbed a jar of water. Servants rushed by him with more jars of water and spadefuls of dirt to douse the flames.

inally, Jing Jing, who had stationed herself near the top of the wall, announced that the soldiers were laying down their crossbows.

"We were too good for them!" the warlord's son crowed. "They could not burn us out!"

The next morning, the soldiers pounded against the gates, intimidating the people in the palace with cruel threats.

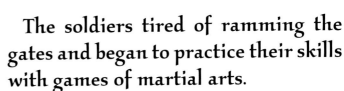

Chuan stirred the vat of spring water, bark, and straw. It would be days before the bark and straw fermented and could be heated and pounded into pulp.

He wondered if the palace wall would stand that long. He began to grind pinewood soot for the artist's ink.

The soldiers tired of ramming the gates and began to practice their skills with games of martial arts.

Jing Jing sat and whittled bamboo flutes while Chuan mixed soot with glue and drops of water. Sometimes she stopped and blew softly into the bamboo. Her breath made the flutes sing a sad, minor note. The mournful sound sent chills down the back of Chuan's neck.

"Do you have to do that?" he asked.
She nodded and gave him a mysterious little smile.

Chuan decided he wouldn't mind working extra hard to make more paper for the artist. "If you stop, I will measure the paper for your kites," he said.

Jing Jing laughed. "We will need the paper to be cut six hands high and six hands wide."

Chuan dipped his hand in some ink he had mixed. Pressing his hand onto a sheet of paper, he printed six handprints up its length. Then, starting again on the first print, he printed six handprints across its width. "We need thirty-six square 'hands' of paper for a kite," he said. "We multiply length times width."

Jing Jing's face creased with a frown. "I don't understand," she murmured.

Chuan dipped his hand again and printed more handprints, until he had six lines of six, completing the square.

She clapped her hands and then counted all thirty-six handprints.

"I have trusted you enough to measure my master's valuable paper. Before I cut it, you must tell me your plan."

Her eyes sparkled. "Do you trust me so much, or are you happy to have something to take your mind off the soldiers?"

The warlord's son stood in the doorway, laughing. "The girl is right again." He dropped an armful of bamboo sticks and spools of string by the sheets of paper. "Show us this clever plan of yours."

Following Jing Jing's instructions, they made three kites. From her robe, she drew three bamboo flutes. She tied one to the head of each kite. "My father, the puppet master, once studied to take the government examination. He has taught me much of our history. Tonight we will use the secret of a Han dynasty emperor."

By the time darkness came, all was in readiness. A slight breeze blew clouds over the moon.

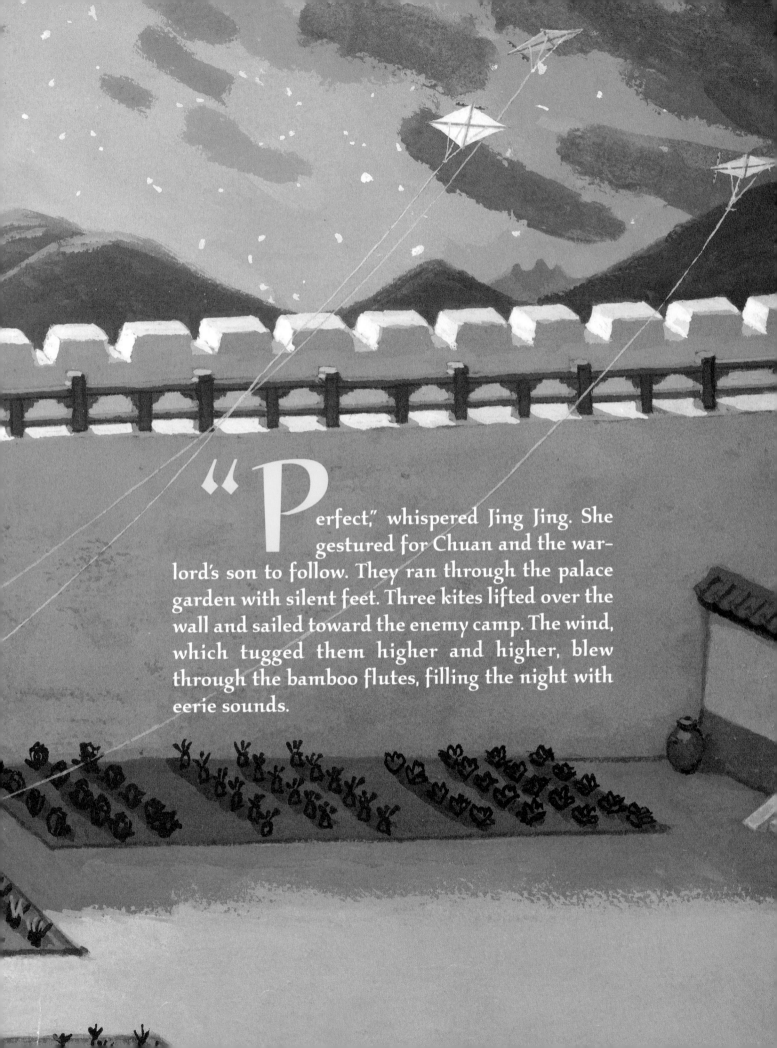

"Perfect," whispered Jing Jing. She gestured for Chuan and the warlord's son to follow. They ran through the palace garden with silent feet. Three kites lifted over the wall and sailed toward the enemy camp. The wind, which tugged them higher and higher, blew through the bamboo flutes, filling the night with eerie sounds.

"Ghosts! Ghosts!" Soldiers' terrified shouts rose from the enemy camp. The children could hear men scrambling around. Then they heard the thundering war horses stampede away.

"The old trick still works," Jing Jing said as she peeked over the palace wall and watched the marauding army flee.

When the returning warlord heard the story, he reached into his pack and found precious coins to reward Chuan and his friends. "Someday," the warlord said, "I must take you three clever children to meet the emperor."

You may have watched a colorful Chinese kite soar in the sky. Stories about kites appear in Chinese literature dating back to 500 B.C. People flew kites for military purposes, to ensure good fortune, and simply for fun. With the Tang dynasty development of a ten-step process to make fine paper, kites became lighter and more beautiful. *Nine Chapters on the Mathematical Art*, the book Chuan mentions, is the oldest surviving Chinese math book. Its first chapter includes finding the areas of plane figures, such as squares, rectangles, triangles, trapezoids, and circles.

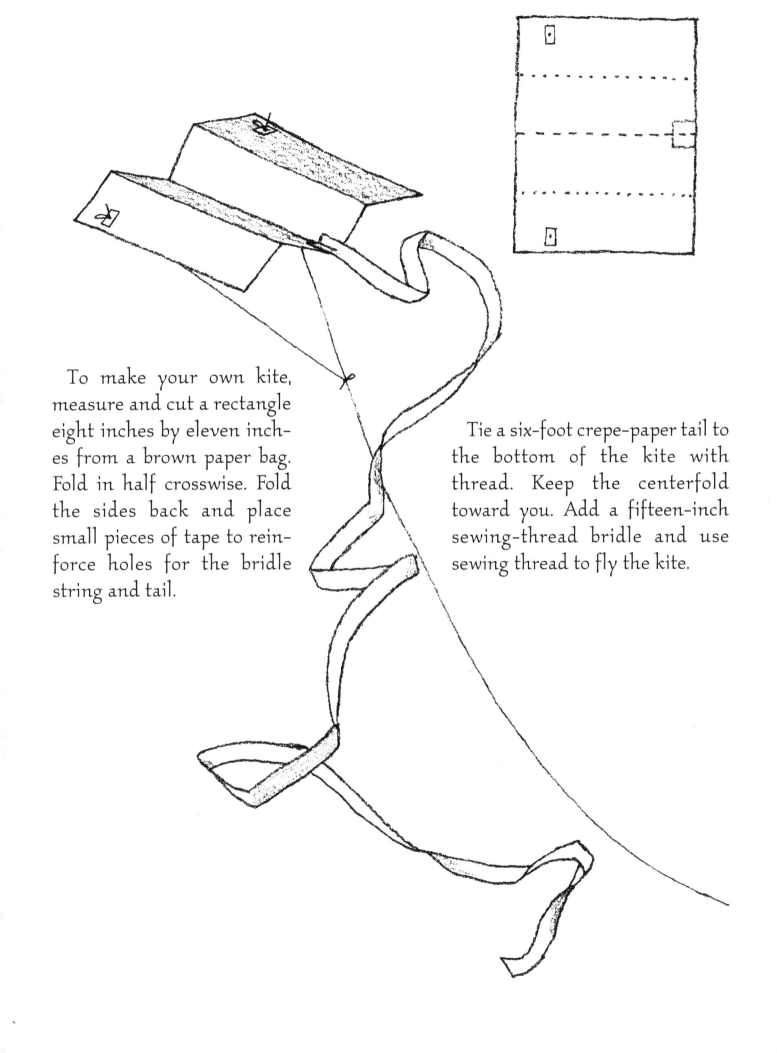

To make your own kite, measure and cut a rectangle eight inches by eleven inches from a brown paper bag. Fold in half crosswise. Fold the sides back and place small pieces of tape to reinforce holes for the bridle string and tail.

Tie a six-foot crepe-paper tail to the bottom of the kite with thread. Keep the centerfold toward you. Add a fifteen-inch sewing-thread bridle and use sewing thread to fly the kite.